D1288153

Pet Dogs
UP CLOSE

by Erika L. Shores

Gail Saunders-Smith, PhD, Consulting Editor

CAPSTONE PRESS
a capstone imprint

Pebble Plus

Pebble Plus is published by Capstone Press,
1710 Roe Crest Drive, North Mankato, Minnesota 56003
www.capstonepub.com

Library of Congress Cataloging-in-Publication Data
Shores, Erika L., 1976–
Pet Dogs Up Close.
pages cm.—(Pebble Plus. Pets Up Close)
Includes bibliographical references and index.
Summary: "Full-color, zoomed-in photos and simple text describe pet dogs' body parts"—Provided by publisher.
Audience: Ages 5-8.
Audience: Grades K to 3.
ISBN 978-1-4914-0583-3 (hardcover : alk. paper)
ISBN 978-1-4914-0617-5 (ebook pdf : alk. paper)
1. Dogs—Juvenile literature. I. Title.
SF426.5.S52 2014
636.7—dc23
2014012292

Editorial Credits
Jeni Wittrock, editor; Bobbie Nuytten, designer; Svetlana Zhurkin, media researcher; Katy LaVigne, production specialist

Photo Credits
Shutterstock: Ann Precious (paw prints), back cover and throughout, colors, cover (background), Eric Isselee, 1, esbobeldijk, 11, Inna Astakhova, 19, Marcel Jancovic, 9, Pavel Hlystov, cover, Piotr Zajac, 15, Rita Kochmarjova, 5, Roland Ijdema, 7, stuart.renneberg, 13, tsik, 17, Volodymyr Burdiak, 21

Note to Parents and Teachers

The Pets Up Close set supports national science standards related to life science. This book describes and illustrates pet dogs. The images support early readers in understanding the text. The repetition of words and phrases helps early readers learn new words. This book also introduces early readers to subject-specific vocabulary words, which are defined in the Glossary section. Early readers may need assistance to read some words and to use the Table of Contents, Glossary, Read More, Internet Sites, and Index sections of the book.

Printed in the United States of America in North Mankato, Minnesota
042014   008087CGF14

Table of Contents

Daring Doggies

Check out those daring dogs!

Dogs have body parts that sniff,

chew, and zoom. Let's take

an up-close look at our playful

four-legged friends.

Noses

Sniff! Sniff!

Dogs use their noses to learn about the world. A dog can smell at least 10,000 times better than a person can.

Ears

Some dog ears are big and tall.

Other ears are long and droopy.

Dogs hear very high sounds

that people can't hear.

Eyes

Dogs' eyes see movement very well. They don't see as many colors as people see. Dogs can see yellow and blue.

Teeth

Dogs bite and chew
with 42 teeth. Hunting dogs
pick up downed birds.
Playful dogs grab toys.

Fur

Pet a dog's soft and curly coat.

Feel another dog's smooth and shiny coat.

Fur keeps dogs warm.

Legs

It's a blur of fur! Strong legs help hunting dogs catch prey. The fastest dog is a greyhound, reaching up to 43 miles (69 kilometers) per hour.

Paws

Look at those puppy paws!
Dog paws have four claws
to dig and scratch. Each front
paw has a fifth claw called
a dewclaw.

dewclaw

Tails

Dogs use their tails
for balance as they run.

Wag, wag!
A wagging tail means
your dog is happy.

Glossary

balance—to keep steady and not fall over

blur—something that can't be seen clearly

coat—an animal's hair or fur

curly—curved or twisted

dewclaw—the inner claw on a dog's front foot; sometimes people have a dog's dewclaws removed

downed—something that has fallen

prey—an animal hunted by other animals for food

wag—to wiggle back and forth

zoom—to run or move quickly

Read More

Dickmann, Nancy. *A Dog's Life.* Watch It Grow. Chicago: Heinemann, 2011.

Hutmacher, Kimberly M. *I Want a Dog. I Want a Pet.* Mankato, Minn.: Capstone Press, 2012.

Slade, Suzanne. *Why Do Dogs Drool?: And Other Questions Kids Have about Dogs.* Kids' Questions. Mankato, Minn.: Picture Window Books, 2010.

Internet Sites

FactHound offers a safe, fun way to find Internet sites related to this book. All of the sites on FactHound have been researched by our staff.

Here's all you do:

Visit www.facthound.com

Type in this code: 9781491405833

Index

Word Count: 196
Grade: 1
Early-Intervention Level: 16